Dear 25

NYASIA DRAPER

All rights reserved.
No part of this publication may be reproduced,
stored or transmitted in any form or by any means, electronic,
mechanical, photocopying, recording, scanning, or otherwise
without written permission from the publisher.
It is illegal to copy this book, post it to a website,
or distribute it by any other means without permission.

ISBN: 978-0-692-15215-7

For you
and me

PREFACE

Thank you! I'm not a known writer nor am I a celebrity, but here you are. There isn't erotica within these pages and no, I am not going to tell you the secrets to winning the lottery. What I will tell you, within these pages, is how I found truth in denial. I will bridge gaps between the young and the old, the unwed and the wed, the procreators and those without child, and parent and child.

Hopefully.

I wrote this book instead of going to therapy. You can decide if that was a good choice later on in the book and get back to me. I encourage you to reach out — good, bad or indifferent.

This is my confessional.

This is a random day when I felt overwhelmed by

my own thoughts and the only person I could talk to was you — the stranger who couldn't talk back.

You need this book. Not because I want commercial success — fuck that. You need this book because it is important to check up on your strong friends, acknowledge the importance of mental health and find success in your failures. You need this book because if the previous sentence doesn't apply to you, it applies to someone close to you and they are too prideful to speak on their sufferings.

Every day I told a lie. Sometimes it was intentional. Other times it wasn't. Both times I felt the person asking the question wasn't worthy of my honesty or I was just not interested in telling the truth.

The question was, "how are you?"

CHAPTER 1

By now, my salary should be $65,000 per year. By now, I should have a place of my own and someone to share it with. By now, we should be engaged. I'm 25 years old. I should have my life together by now, right? Wrong. By now, I've realized that scheduling my life was my first mistake and hating myself for it would be my last.

Like many, I imagined adulthood to be filled with love, family, financial freedom and excitement. I was going to have life mastered by the time I was 25 years old in hopes of maximizing my time to enjoy it. Every day wouldn't be fireworks and funnel cakes, but I would have the means to make it so.

Flashback to me at 17 years old. I became what I called an optimistic pessimist. I had it quoted on a chalkboard wall decal in my college dorm and I loved watching people underestimate its truths. An optimistic pessimist is a person who was optimistic negative things would happen in hopes of preparing for it. The perspective allowed the individual to prepare for negative outcomes in hopes of weakening the impact of disappointment. I can admit that this viewpoint has rubbed some the wrong way, but I stand by my choice. I developed this sense of realism from a state of pain.

My father abandoned me so I adopted the notion that if my own father can turn his back on me, I'm sure the world is capable of doing the same. His absence taught me not to have high expectations of others. Titles like "father" don't dictate the actions of a man. Therefore, people shouldn't be held accountable by their titles, rather by their actions.

I've tried to explain my optimistic pessimistic perspective in a way that conveyed a proactive spirit, but once people hear the term "pessimistic" they no longer listen. I found strength in not expecting much of people. I never expected my perspective to be accepted or rejected. It was just how my mind rewired itself when my dad left. I made the mistake of discussing my perspective during a job interview with Apple. I'm certain my optimistic pessimistic viewpoint, tangent on how religion was introduced to me as an obligation, and multiple follow-up calls was the reason I was blackballed from the company.

I applied to be a specialist. Not because I had a passion for Apple's technology, but because it was a high-paying job that gave me enough leeway to focus on my true passion, writing. As a teen, one of my fears was having to transfer schools or change majors and lose credits in the process. I hated wasting time so I needed to do everything in my power to get into a good college.

I knew from early on I wanted to be a writer. In high school I participated in extracurricular activities that would help me fulfill that dream. I needed to secure my spot in a writing-intensive program that was affordable and offered flexibility in my career. I didn't want my degree to be too specific. For example, if I got a degree in medical copywriting and discovered it wasn't a good fit for me, I would have to go back to school in order to change professions.

Seems a bit career driven for a teenager, but I was determined to fulfill the promises I made to myself — become a writer at a reputable publication, obtain financial stability, move into the perfect home and start creating a family by age 25.

I didn't account for the experiences I would later learn to value like visiting Chichén Itzá in Mexico, dorming in college, or enjoying a solo, uninterrupted lunch in a greenhouse. I didn't think about the possibility of loving the wrong person, but being thankful for the lessons the failed relationship taught me. I never thought I would question my career choices or think the picture I painted of adulthood was more fantasy than reality. I was focused on the masterpiece with little to no room for small portraits.

My social life was just background noise I listened to when my mother allowed it. My mother wasn't strict, she was careful. It only annoyed me when I wanted to do something within the hour and she "had to think about it" or told me no "because [I] said so."

Sidebar: Logically answering your children isn't a sign of submission, folks. Sometimes answering a "why not?" is a good opportunity to teach your children your train of thought and give them clarity for future decisions.

If I couldn't run the streets, as my mother would say, because of her carefulness, it was because I had to hold the household down. While my mother was at work, I did housework, made dinner, and helped my brothers with their homework. There was a male figure that could've done the same, but let's just say I was more reliable. That was our dynamic, my mother and I. We are and will always be a team. No matter who was around at the time or what was happening in our lives, we tackled life together.

My father hated that. He just wanted his baby girl to be his baby girl. "That's not your responsibility," he'd say. "Your job is to be a child. That's it!"

My parents split when I was young. Religious Caribbean parents' troubled, loving teen meets American basketball-playing, car enthusiast. Together they discovered lust and had me. The end.

Of course there are stories in between that time that sometimes spill into day-to-day life like my grandparents kicking my mother out when she was pregnant with me and my father never having a positive father figure of his own, but this is about my quarter-life crisis, not how my family dynamic shaped me into a socially awkward overachiever. M'kay?

I don't want to dive too much in to my family dynamics because it can easily turn into a battle of perspectives. Although, it is the foundation of my being, their stories are not mine to tell. My perspective may begin a dialogue I am not ready to have outside of these pages and I am at peace with my truth.

Outside of parental interference, my social life wasn't a priority to me. Luckily, I was able to develop lifelong friendships with a group of girls from my junior high school. Their names are Kimberly, Jennifer and Nikisha. The names are listed in the order that I met them. They are the pettiest women I know so it is important that I note that. Together we are OTF; Only the Family.

We treated our birthdays like holidays. When my 25th birthday was approaching, we treated it no different. OTF and I spoke briefly about my lack of enthusiasm for the occasion, but they didn't take it well when I told them I really didn't want to celebrate my birthday. My friends and I had a group chat. It's how we stayed in touch and maintained our friendship no matter what direction life pulled us in.

"What do you want to do for your birthday?" asked Jennifer.

"I'm thinking about going bowling and just a little dinner," I answered.

"Bowling and dinner is cool and all, but I'mma need your big two-five to require some twerking."

"Facts," said Kimberly in agreeance.

I laughed at those messages, but was slightly annoyed. Just last week we agreed a quarter-life crisis is something everyone ignores, but it's tearing away at our sanity. We all had a plan for our future, but those plans were destroyed by naivety, a terrible job market, a fickle housing market and unhealthy relationships.

Your birthday is supposed to be a celebration of years of accomplishments and perseverance. The fuck was I celebrating? My ability to still be alive?

I wasn't in the field of study that Sallie Mae was billing me for, I still had to ask my mother for permission to have company over and I haven't traveled much. I didn't have much to celebrate.

This wasn't the 25 I had hoped for.

There I was, 25 years old and my life hadn't even started. I'd accomplished so little and I'd been nowhere. I was in a healthy relationship, but making my parents grandparents was out of the question. My life was nothing like I dreamed it would be and I felt empty inside. Not the type of emptiness that results in deep depression and substance abuse, but the type of emptiness that leads to group chat rants and indecisive boredom.

I was having a quarter-life crisis.

CHAPTER 2

When I was 22 years old, I started questioning if I made the right choice in pursuing a career in writing. I did my research on the industry and gained all of the necessary requirements:

Bachelors of Science in Professional Communications, minor in English Literature.

Two years of experience as an editor in chief of my college paper.

Two internships at popular publications: Maxim and Russel Simmons' Global Grind.

Over a dozen bylines in news, politics and entertainment.

But, I didn't receive any decent job offers. Sure, I got the typical marketing opportunity, but did I really want to run around Manhattan pitching office supplies? It would cost me more money to travel from Long Island, where I lived, to Manhattan than the salary they would offer.

I began doubting myself. Maybe I wasn't as good of a writer as I thought. Maybe I spent all this time honing a craft that wasn't a fit for me.

I've heard successful entertainment professionals say if you are passionate about something then you should be willing to do it for free. Although I agree with the sentiment, debt collectors don't give two shits about your aspirations in life.

I could hear the clock ticking. I was running out of time.

With every ticktock on my life's clock, I could see pieces of my fantasized world crumbling at the feet of each disappointment. To my family and friends I was overreacting. To me, I was face-to-face with mediocrity.

I traveled through life anticipating this moment. I didn't find joy in graduating from high school because graduating from college was the ultimate goal. Life after college is where I expected to find my joy. It's where I expected to pat myself on the back and reap the rewards of my hard work. I didn't anticipate developing self-doubt and hopelessness.

Thankfully I secured a remote, freelance writing position weeks before college graduation. It was only for a month, but it gave me bylines in various beats. From Justin Bieber's legal issues to the discovery of a woman living solely off sunlight, I was racking up bylines and enjoying morning cartoons. It was an ideal situation.

I wasn't the best writer out there. My inability to secure full-time employment prior to this opportunity solidified that. My vocabulary was limited, my editing skills were subpar, but my syntax was solid. I'm one of those writers who never drafted their projects. My professors always told me my writing has the potential to be phenomenal if I would just triple check my work. The idea of editing didn't set in until later on.

I was confident that I would be offered to transition from freelancer to full-time staff writer because my editor never showed any signs of dissatisfaction with my work. I expected to be hired, but I didn't anticipate the lack of professionalism associated with the process.

I walked into the office prepared to negotiate a contract and secure a full-time position. Instead, I was met with a verbal offer that didn't include any benefits. I was aware that the company wasn't large enough to offer me the bells and whistles, but I was expecting a minimum of an explanation of my position in writing. When I questioned the accuracy of the information presented to me I was told "I'll email everything to you. In the meantime, you can still write and we'll pay you per post."

Excuse me?

You want me to continue to provide you with 10 posts a day and drive traffic to your website because you verbally agreed to pay me per post? Yea, they had me fucked up.

I asked for my terms in writing and confirmation of an extension on my freelancing contract. Days went by and follow-up emails were left unanswered.

In my final follow-up email, I thanked the company for their time and ended our business relationship. It wasn't until then that I got a reply. There was nothing they could say that would change my mind. Instead of being an employed writer, I became a full-time hermit instead.

That's right. I went nowhere, did nothing, and ate everything as I wore out my mother's couch and became allergic to sunlight. I cried randomly. Everything I could not do spiraled into thoughts that I was going to become exactly what I feared — a statistic.

According to the Economic Policy Institute, 9.4 percent of young, black, college graduates are unemployed in comparison to 4.7 percent of white college students as of February 2016. The overall underemployment rate is at 12.6 percent in comparison to 9.6 percent in the previous year. The percentages depicts a job market that isn't receptive to young, black, college graduates. It also proves that the jobs that are available are least likely to utilize the skills developed while obtaining college degrees. When discussing the unemployment rate in America or the state of the job market, politicians focus on those who are not educated or well versed in the markets they apply for. Those of us who are within the underemployment umbrella aren't even mentioned.

Nyasia Draper

Everything around me turned into a reminder of not only the statistics I was up against, but the stigma of what my unemployment represented. Being unemployed meant those who told me not to get a degree in communications were right. Being unemployed meant more time living by other people's rules. Being unemployed made me feel powerless.

When I got stuck on the Long Island Rail Road because a conductor abandoned his station I thought "if you would've got your dream job fresh out of college you would have your own car by now, but you don't. You're a bum."

When my little brother stole my blanket and used it as a mop I thought, "If you did what you were supposed to do you would have your own apartment filled with blankets, but you don't. You ain't shit."

When I searched for jobs that aligned with my educational and professional background, the maximum salary was $35,000. I thought, "Your dumb ass just had to fall in love with writing right? You thought communication was key and now you ain't got no keys to your own house, brokie!"

DEAR 25

My mother didn't pressure me to get off my ass and get a job because she knew the amount of pressure I put on myself. She encouraged me to trust the process and not to doubt myself because the schedule I had in place wasn't working. "You can't plan for everything," she said. It was her favorite line. The more she said it, the angrier it made me.

It infuriated me that everyone around me tried to define what success should mean to me. Telling me what I should be happy with was irritating. I made my loved ones proud and that's cool, but no one cared that I wasn't proud of *myself.*

No one asked me if I was proud of myself. They only told me I should be. I was always being told how to feel.

"You should be proud of yourself. You graduated on time."

"You should be happy. You got a gig fresh out of college."

"You should enjoy this moment and be excited for the future."

"You live rent free. You should enjoy it."

The accomplishments I made were a mere checklist

to me and a cause for celebration for others. I set the bar high for myself. My standards were not dictated by what others thought I was capable of. I wanted more for myself and everyone kept telling me I'd done enough.

It was the first time I felt inadequate.

CHAPTER 3

A few months went by. A few months of depression, being unproductive and weight gain. Finally, I got tired of feeling sorry for myself and contacted a hiring agency for employment. I applied to become an underwriting assistant through the agency, assuming it was a corporate communications job that would give me the experience I needed to bring the schedule I had for my life back to fruition.

The recruiter went over my resume and was excited that I had a writing background. He told me the future in underwriting was lucrative and that he was positive this would be a great opportunity to explore my options in the corporate world.

Nyasia Draper

When I went on the job interview I was prepared to secure a favorable salary.

Despite popular opinion, college did prepare me for this moment. I arrived with copies of my resume, in business casual attire, and I researched the company just as I would in preparation to interview a subject for an article.

People fail to realize that an interview is open ended. You are being interviewed for the applied position and you are interviewing the company to see if the company is a good fit for you. The key is to give them the illusion that they are controlling the conversation when in fact it's give and take.

The recruiter and the hiring manager of the company clearly did not discuss what the job description was. I walked in optimistic and walked out confused. This was not the job I signed up for, but it was one I was going to take.

The hiring manager questioned my intentions because my resume reeked of aspiring journalist. Thanks to that good ol' college education, I was able to reroute the conversation and convince her that being an underwriting assistant was a part of my career goals. Within days, I was offered a temporary, full-time position which later became permanent.

I utilized my communications degree to provide support to medical stop-loss insurance agents, notify the insured of requirements, manage accounts, and issue policies and cancellation notices. I didn't plan on exploring the insurance field, but it was working for me. I developed an appreciation for the industry and began to reschedule my life around it.

Although I still wanted to be a writer, I began mapping out my future with underwriting as my guide. The recruiter was right. It was a lucrative industry that could grant me access to being a corporate communications manager at a Fortune 500 company. With enough years of experience and my degree in communications, I was confident in my new future.

The more I dedicated to medical stop-loss insurance the more I felt myself falling out of love with writing. The passion was gone. I was heartbroken when blank pages no longer inspired me. Writing became a reminder of what once was. It's painful falling out of love with the one thing you had undeniable faith in.

I was once a poetic dreamer and now I've become a corporate hopeful.

At 23 years old, I was back on track. It was another victory in the "I told you I can plan my life" chronicles. I felt accomplished. I bought my first car, a 2012 Volkswagen Jetta GLI Autobahn — don't ever call it a Jetta though. My love life was going smoothly, my friends were still that — friends, and my family was intact.

I just reconnected with my father after five years. My parents fought for visitation rights and my father lost the case because I told the judge I wanted to visit him whenever I wanted. I strongly believed a court order would only complicate things. If my father was guaranteed visitation every Saturday and I decided one Saturday I didn't want to go, it would put my mother in violation of a court order. I didn't want to put my mother in an awkward position nor did I want my relationship with my father to be manufactured by a judge.

My father wanted me to live with him, but I always

felt like a stranger in his house. I always felt like being myself would only disappoint him. I wasn't a girly girl like his wife nor was I a lover of sports like his stepson. I was a little rough around the edges and I enjoyed writing poetry. I didn't fit in.

His wife and my mother were always at odds. My stepmother felt my father was too lenient with me. It always felt like it was her versus me. It was as if my father's love for me somehow threatened their relationship.

I will never forget the time she was mad that I almost ate an entire box of cereal. It was the middle of the day and no one had gone food shopping yet. So, I'd been hitting the cereal all day. With milk, without milk — cereal was in a bowl, on my lap, being enjoyed. When my stepmother reached for the cereal, she was mad there wasn't much left. I admitted to the "crime" and stood in silence as she berated me.

"Cereal is for breakfast," she said.

"It's the middle of the day and you're reaching for cereal to eat for lunch. A bit of a contradiction. Don't you think?" I thought.

That incident stuck with me. It still annoys me till this day. How petty do you have to be to pick a fight with a child over cereal? And not just any child, one that is obsessed with food.

I couldn't let that court order be granted.

Instead of speaking to me about my reasoning, my father abandoned me. He thought he was doing me a favor. At least that's what he told me. I think he was tired of the back and forth with my mother. He thought my testimony would be the end to his suffering, but instead I decided to end mine. It wasn't until we reconnected that my assumptions were confirmed.

I was supposed to go into the court room and make it better for him. I thought I did. Instead, the judge took my refusal to put visitation restrictions in writing as my father selfishly requesting changes. She somehow interpreted my fear of legal documentation to me not wanting more time with my father. He felt his baby girl didn't love him as much as she said she did. Ironic — because I was thinking the same thing.

Witnessing my parents fight over me was exhausting. So much so that I never wished for them to get back together. I was never the kid who fantasized about their parents falling back in love. I knew early on they were incompatible.

My father wasn't aware that his absence would create an emotionally disheveled adult. Till this day he doesn't know he was the only man to ever break my heart. When we reconnected I told him his actions were inexcusable. I didn't tell my father he single-handedly created my pessimistic spirit because I didn't want to hurt him.

Imagine that. He was the one in the wrong and I still felt obligated to protect him.

With all avenues of my life in order, I focused on my career in insurance. Underwriting was still my focus, but I tried to rekindle the old flame that was writing by freelancing. I interviewed Power 105.1's Charlamagne Tha God and had it published in Sister 2 Sister. It was my first time being published in a magazine.

I was on cloud nine.

I thought the opportunity would open the door to more celebrity interviews, recognition, and finally putting my degree to proper use. As quick as the article was published was as quick as it was forgotten. I tried to land other interviews and pitch ideas to no avail. The magazine filed for bankruptcy and my window of opportunity was closed.

I'm thankful for the high Sister 2 Sister gave me. A short-lived high, but appreciated. It was a testament that when the unexpected happens, it isn't a cause for concern. It simply means you've been redirected and how you handle it will determine your final destination. The publication gave me the reassurance I needed to continue writing.

For years I thought I was a terrible writer people tolerated because of my determination. The Charlamagne interview received a great response from not only Charlamagne, but his social media followers who read the article thanks to his cosign. I've gotten good feedback before, but not from an influencer and certainly not in the midst of self-doubt.

This reassurance gave me a clean slate. I quit doubting myself and in that moment I realized how much effort I put into my career without putting effort into living my life. I had tunnel vision. There is truth in the quote "to live doesn't mean you're alive."

The lack of memories I had that wasn't associated with professional success, proved I was dead for the majority of my life. I did nothing but watch the world pass me by as I tried to keep my schedule afloat.

The sentiment was emphasized as I drunkenly took a step back and looked at a bar filled with my friends. We were at Tonic in Times Square celebrating my 23rd birthday. I had a career, my car and insurance was in my name, my credit score was astonishing, and my skin was clear. We were there to celebrate me. I finally felt *deserving* of a celebration.

I felt good. I felt *alive*.

Sort of like a born-again Christian. You know, someone granted another chance at life by obtaining clarity through religion, life experiences or a self-help book.

I realized I was more than an aspiring writer, aspiring mother and aspiring wife. I found myself within the confines of my fear of failure. I was an empty vessel traveling through life strategizing my moves for the next five years, but I didn't even know what I wanted for dinner.

I've experienced happiness, but I wasn't happy.

They say the best way to evaluate your life is to picture your life flashing before your eyes. If you like what you see, you're living your truth. If you don't, make changes. I didn't want to be on my death bed and have nothing to watch.

I didn't want the people in my life to feel like pawns in my chess game of success. I wanted to be able to sit in a room with my own thoughts and smile. I'm talking about a grin-from-ear-to-ear-with-joy-in-my-heart type of smile. It was the type of smile my grandfather, Elijah, had.

I took this epiphany and made changes. I planned trips with my friends, I went out for dinner during a work week and I even began to take more pictures. I was being optimistic for once. There were no "what ifs" anymore, just what was. I was focused on living for today without sacrificing my tomorrows.

It was short lived, but worth every second.

Everything felt different. My laugh was hearty and

I ate to experience different flavors rather than shift my emotions. The people around me changed, too. They seemed happier. Perhaps, the stress of dealing with me and my many panic attacks weighed heavier on them than I thought. Maybe, I never truly got a chance to see them for who they were because I was too busy preparing for who I could be.

I found my happiness — or so I thought.

CHAPTER 4

Every day was predictable. Wake up, go to work, argue with the oldest lady in my department, use my lunch break to complain to my boyfriend about said old hag, go home to cook, bathe and repeat the next day. I was bored out of my damn mind, but had no energy or inspiration to change it. I was definitely in a be-careful-what-you-wish-for situation.

The schedule I had for my livelihood was set in motion and I was in the doldrums.

This is what I wanted. A reliable career and people that loved me. There was no drama, no instability and no sadness. I had what I was fighting for and still felt unfulfilled.

I felt like a soccer mom during off-season; aimlessly trying to occupy my time.

What were my hobbies? Why couldn't I find solace in writing anymore? What the hell is going on with my wardrobe? I felt like I let myself go physically and metaphorically.

I was so caught up in setting up my future that my present became dull and repetitive. I knew what the future me wanted, but the current me was confused. I wasn't Nyasia anymore. I was back to being *just* someone's friend, someone's girlfriend, someone's daughter, someone's sister and so on. Only now, I've added underwriting assistant to the mix.

I found a spark when I realized I was financially stable enough to buy a home. I'd been apartment hunting for quite some time when I got a call from an apartment complex. I was approved for a unit and it was time to start the move-in process. I was on a two-year wait list, so when I got the call I was excited.

"Come in and we'll take your deposit and you can pick out your apartment Ms. Draper," said the property manager.

It was the change my boring life needed. It was a step

closer to undeniable independence and officially becoming an adult.

I gathered the updated paperwork they requested, left work early and headed to pick out my new apartment. I was familiar with the property thanks to a prior walk-through, but this time around, I got to choose what floor I wanted to be on and a specific floor plan.

Before I arrived I put some furniture and household items in an online shopping cart just to ensure I accounted for any unexpected moving expenses. I wanted my place to be a reflection of who I was, past and present, with a relaxed, yet inviting feel. That meant tons of family photos, soothing candles, a meme wall because — life, and the softest towels I've ever felt. I wanted my place to be everything I didn't have in a home. Not to say my current living arrangement was subpar, but it wasn't *mine*.

I learned quickly that the unexpected expense would be wasted time. After glancing at my updated paperwork, I was denied the apartment for the agreed price, $1,050 to $1,350 per month with a two percent annual increase.

DEAR 25

The apartment complex was income based which is why my rental price was explained in ranges. The rent amount I was approved for was based on old bank statements. I started working part time at a local Best Buy to prepare for my new apartment. The extra income put me above the allowed income limit for subsidized housing.

The rental price for my "new" income would be $1,600. Even though I explained the temporary increase in my income, I was told "We figured if you could do it once, you can do it again. Therefore, it counts towards your application." I expressed my disappointment and professionally told the housing manager to kiss my ass.

That's mortgage money. Why would I pay someone $1,600 in rent just so I can be assed out whenever they decided to increase the rent or deny my lease renewal? Fuck that.

The price was in line with other rental properties that provided similar amenities, but it was still unreasonable. The school district was rated a three out of ten, the crime rate was alarming, and the location was underdeveloped.

Instead of dwelling on the disappointment, I applied for a home loan and was approved for $100,000 soon after. To some that wasn't much. Growing up, the adults made homeownership seem impossible.

"If you want homeownership, get out of New York," they'd say.

Leaving New York wasn't an option. I equated moving out of New York to taking the easy way out or giving up. If I could buy a home in New York it would be more satisfying because I made it in a city people deemed impossible to survive in.

New York was home. Nowhere comforted me like New York did. I was born and raised in Brooklyn; moved to Long Island in college. I have an attachment to New York that I can't shake. I refused to give up on the place that made me. I wanted to earn my keep — feel me?

It's melodramatic, but it's how I felt. Besides, if you could make it in New York that meant you're capable of anything. I'd much rather reside in a state that challenges me to reach my full potential than a state that hands success to me on a platter.

If I didn't do my research, I too would think all homes were well over $300,000. No one taught me the difference between condominiums, cooperatives (co-ops), single-family homes, and multi-family homes. I was never taught the tax benefits of homeownership and what percentage of a mortgage was needed towards a down payment. With the help of a local realtor, I searched far and wide for the perfect property.

After months of searching, I had everything I needed and picked out the perfect co-op. The listing price was $90,000. The housing association fee would be approximately $350 per month and the owners were willing to pay my housing association fees for five months. My mortgage, including housing association fees, would be $950.

$950 would make me a homeowner. There would be no chance of an unexplained rent increase, there were no income restrictions, and I had the power to turn my home into an income property.

Becoming a landlord was important to me. It was more than just my retirement plan. It was my way of giving back to the community. Growing up, I hated all of my landlords. They didn't take care of the properties, were extremely invasive and the properties were overpriced.

As I got older, finding a place was a struggle without having the $60,000 per year salary I imagined in my teens. I wanted to be the change I wanted to see by creating affordable and attractive housing. The co-op was a step in that direction.

My realtor took me for a walk-through of the property not knowing my mind was already made up. The viewing was just a formality. To me, I was home. As he explained the perks of the property, I allowed myself to envision my life there.

"There's a double vanity in the bathroom," he said.

"Perfect for when I resell," I thought.

Without hesitation, I made an offer. I was confident in my offer because I offered $5,000 more than the listing price. It wasn't much, but it's what I had.

"Dad, the co-op needs a new kitchen, but I priced it all out," I said.

"Don't worry about any of that. Daddy will take care of everything. Just let me know when everything is finalized and I will come up and handle it," he replied.

My father lives in Georgia. He's retired and obsessed with home improvement. I was reluctant to let him lend a helping hand because I have issues accepting assistance from people. I also wasn't sure if his offer was because he wanted to be a helpful father or because he hadn't been one for five years. It's my Achilles heel and the reason for most of my anxiety.

I always viewed the need for assistance as a handicap. I had the superwoman syndrome and my paranoia of outside help being thrown in my face caused a lot of stress. Learning that needing help and accepting help doesn't make me less than was a hard lesson I'm still trying to come to terms with.

It was happening again. That feeling of euphoria when everything was going as planned. This was my moment. This was all a part of the schedule. I was going to be a 24-year-old homeowner.

The longer it took for the realtor to update me on

the status of my offer, the more I envisioned my life in the co-op. I planned out game nights and created a grocery list. I was confident I was moments away from having my own place.

Then the damn realtor called and told me I lost the co-op to a cash offer. Who the fuck is walking around with $95,000 in cash?

I'll tell you who — developers and immigrants. Developers have an unreasonable amount of cash on hand because in this industry cash offers trump mortgage loans. With a cash offer, the seller or the bank gets their money up front without the risk of the buyer potentially being unable to maintain the mortgage payments. As for the immigrants, you have to be living and working in the United States for two years before applying for a home loan.

A cash offer also eliminates the need for good credit. Good credit, bad credit or no credit doesn't matter because there is no need for a mortgage loan.

I'm sure there are other scenarios, but these are the reasons that were presented to me at the time.

I was pissed, but I wasn't crushed. It was a smart

business move. One I wish I was in the position to make. It also wasn't the first time I fell in love with a property I couldn't have. This wasn't the first time something unscheduled happened.

At this point in my life, I realized yet another personality flaw. I couldn't focus on obtaining the co-op without visualizing my life there. I was a classic case of counting my chicks before they hatched. Either way, my life experiences taught me how to positively deal with unfavorable outcomes. I'm not sure if it was as a result of me trying to be in control of everything or unhealthy optimism.

I was hopeful for the future and refocused my attention on exploring the potential of advancing my career. There were a few insurance licenses I could obtain that would make me more marketable. I spoke with coworkers who encouraged me to take the courses in hopes of catapulting my rise on the corporate ladder.

One day, I was accessing procedures at work when I got an unexpected call from my boyfriend.

His voice was shallow.

"Babe," he said.

"What happened?" I replied.

There was a brief silence and within that moment the world stopped as if his voice controlled its' axis.

"Larry died."

Without uttering a word, I hung up the phone, sprinted down the aisle of cubicles towards the conference room and interrupted my manager's meeting. I didn't realize my body was shaking until I collapsed in her arms as I said "I have to go. My stepfather just died."

She held me until I realized I was crying in a stranger's arms. I had no clue how my mother was handling his passing and the office wasn't the place to unravel.

I thought I was stoic, but I wasn't. I hated myself for that; allowing people to bear witness to me being emotional. I gave myself a quick pep talk. "Okay, you had a moment. Now, pull it together and go be there for your mother and your brother," I thought. "We don't have time for this."

Fun fact: I never had time for that.

My manager instructed my in-house nemesis to follow me to my car and ensure I didn't drive off. My body was shaking, I couldn't finish my sentences and my eyes couldn't focus on one thing. This felt familiar. This was a panic attack.

My anxiety is a huge hardship for me. The best way I can describe it is my anxiety runs my life, I don't run my life. My body holds me captive whenever I'm feeling negative emotions, try to push towards new experiences or because it feels like it. It's scary when you're overcome by panic and you can feel your mind trying to pinpoint the problem while searching for a solution simultaneously, and your voice echoes "what's happening?" in your head.

My mother told me there was nothing wrong with me. My friends told me everyone has anxiety and it's all in my head. But I wasn't okay. It wasn't the norm and something was and still is very wrong with me.

They don't know that it can take an entire day to recover from an anxiety attack. They don't know it can last for days and there's no cause for most of them. They don't know anxiety has blurred my vision, decreased my appetite, and makes it hard for me to verbalize my thoughts. My words are slurred, I stutter, and at times I felt like I was talking, but nothing was coming out.

I legitimately can't stop my hands from shaking when my anxiety takes over. My friends and family don't care that I have to plan recovery time when invited on adventures that may be out of my comfort zone. They don't care that sometimes crying is the only solution and allowing me to do so in silence is the best thing they could do. They don't think that I am capable of being weak or that my mind tries to analyze and complete tasks in minuets when it should take hours. They don't feel my heart pounding, my mind racing, the shortness of breath or the fear.

My friends and family don't see how dismissive their comments, assumptions and accusations are. My anxiety does not make me incapable and I don't like being reminded that it exists. I feel it, at bay, lurking in my chest. They don't know how it feels to be scared of yourself.

The day Larry died, my anxiety intensified and that intensity lasted for months.

"She can't drive like this. Nyasia, you cannot drive like this," my manager said firmly.

Larry and my mother dated for a little more than a decade. He was the father of my youngest brother and the reason for awkward silences at the dinner table. We didn't agree on key family issues, but he was the shining light in my little brother's eyes and the man my mother vowed to marry.

We weren't on speaking terms when he died.

Larry was an old-school cat. He had a hustler's spirit and lived on his own terms. He paraded around the house drinking soda, smoking cigarettes, and refusing medical help despite him having multiple health issues.

"I'm gon' die anyway. Might as well," he would say.

And he did.

Watching people kill themselves isn't easy. Especially when they have a family desperately begging them to stay alive. It's selfish for them to not consider how their absence would cause trauma and it's selfish for us to ask them to live for us rather than themselves. There are no win-ners in death.

Larry died on his own terms and as selfishly as it seemed, I understood it. In his death I found common ground with the man I couldn't even muster up the respect to greet when I walked in a room.

In his death I learned he was a man who never experienced genuine love and respect. People always wanted something from him. Therefore, he couldn't care less how his actions affected others or how others viewed him. He was in the business of protecting himself and always being the victor in any situation. Debatable, of course, but this is what I got out of his death.

I think about him often. I think of how different things could've been if we communicated better as a family. I think of where my mother would be if he survived. I question how long he would have had if he started dialysis earlier or what type of Christmas tree he would choose only to laugh at us decorating the house for a "regular day."

Larry's death crippled my mother.

I won't go into details on how exactly her world crumbled, but I will tell you my heart shattered putting hers back together. My little brother kept up a good front for a 6-year-old, but when the days turned to nights, he gripped on to my mother in fear that she too would disappear. He was diagnosed with a series of emotional disorders including an attachment disorder.

Larry's death created an attachment disorder so potent, my brother had to be homeschooled and my mother had to take a leave of absence from work.

When she would try to leave the house, my little brother would latch on to her body, scream in pain, begging for her to stay. "Don't leave me, Mommy. Please. PLEASE."

You don't know hopelessness till you looked in the eyes of a 6-year-old who thought every time he saw you was going to be the last time.

Shit killed me. My family was in pain and there was nothing I could do about it.

Larry died in September of 2015, right before the holidays. Not to sound insensitive, but I always thought missing Larry during the holiday season was ironic because he never wanted to participate in holiday activities. It was like pulling teeth to get that man downstairs.

CHAPTER 5

Every day after his death was a challenge. Routines were changed and emotions were high. I could no longer up and leave my mother in the house, alone. It was a process and I'm grateful my job was understanding of that. My focus was always off and my anxiety was causing the type of chaos I wasn't familiar with. Things were rocky and we all needed therapy, but were too proud to get any until my mom decided to lead by example. I've yet to explore that option.

A few months later, my job announced my department and a few others were being let go. Not because of inadequacy, but because of outsourcing. The company decided to end their relationships on Long Island and focus on their New Jersey and Manhattan locations. The decision wasn't unexpected. The company took a huge financial loss overseas and business within my department slowed down drastically.

Some of my coworkers were visibly upset and others, like myself, felt indifferent. This wasn't a concern of mine. My family and I were actively recovering from Larry's death. I can replace a job. I can't replace a person.

I wasn't satisfied with my salary and hadn't been for some time. Being laid off was the push I needed to make an effort to change that.

I decided to forfeit the proposed severance package of four weeks of pay and accept a similar position at a local company. The job description was slightly different, but the increase in pay made the change in responsibilities unnoticeable. With this job I got my own laptop, traveled on the company's dime and made procedural changes within the first few weeks of being hired.

I admit the transition between companies wasn't easy. I was experienced in medical stop-loss insurance, not multiple lines of coverage. My inexperience didn't prove to be an issue nor was it mentioned. My new boss and coworkers assured me I was progressing well. I was sent various "good job" emails and even spoke with my boss about how important I was, a millennial, to the longevity of the company.

His words, not mine.

There I was — traveling back and forth to Texas for training and enjoying my new salary. I hated the job, but I was loving the perks. I made the most of my current situation and tried to retain as much information as I could to keep the position.

Everything was going well. I had all my ducks in a row, but I couldn't silence my inner pessimist. There's never a time where everything is going well and doom isn't a few situations away. Within weeks, doom arrived and she brought misery with her.

My grandfather, Elijah, died.

CHAPTER 6

My grandfather died in Jamaica while I was vacationing in Florida. I was in the middle of a nap when my mother called. Through her yelling I heard "He's in a better place. It is what it is. Don't cry. He lived a good life. That's it," and she hung up.

I could tell she was more angry than sad. It sounded like she decided to build a wall in response to her pain, but as her daughter, I immediately noticed the cracks.

My knees buckled. My chest ached. "Ugh! Why would she call you and tell you that," my boyfriend said.

I would've been pissed if I found out days later so my mother did the right thing. He just felt I was already stressed out and preferred that I would've been able to enjoy my vacation.

Nyasia Draper

I was so confused. It was assumed a fall led to Granddad's death. I don't know where the assumption stemmed from, but his death certificate credited a stroke, high blood pressure and diabetes.

I spent my 25th birthday in Jamaica. I complained the entire time leading up to the trip.

My grandparents didn't have Wi-Fi and used one fan to cool down the whole house. I'd much rather spend my birthday on a resort, but as annoying as I made the upcoming trip seem, I'm glad I used that time to create some memories with my grandfather. I didn't think it would be the last time I saw him alive.

Yes, Granddad was in a wheelchair, couldn't bathe himself and sometimes forgot his own birthday, but he was still Granddad. He still smiled when he saw me. He still yelled at whoever was around to make sure the baby, me, was never hungry.

I thought he had more time.

I replayed the last moments we had together in my mind. The memory that sticks out the most was when Grandma, Granddad and I sat on their veranda in Jamaica. We were all laughing. I don't remember what we were laughing at, but I remember my grandfather's smile.

He was so happy.

It took years for me to visit because I was scared of the outcome. I couldn't fathom going to Jamaica to witness my grandparents declining health and then return to the States. I tried everything to get them to move back to New York.

I looked up properties for them to consider, balanced their budgets to prove the move was financially responsible, and I created a plan that ensured they would get adequate care courtesy of their own family. Still, they chose to stay in Jamaica. It was their decision to choose their homeland over me that ultimately strained our relationship.

I interpreted their refusal to relocate as their version of suicide. They'd rather die in Jamaica than come back to the States to be surrounded by family.

Returning to the States meant better medical treatment, less money spent on shipping barrels of necessities to Jamaica, and my grandparents would be less susceptible to elder abuse. My grandparents have missed the birth of their grandchildren, graduations and the opportunity to strengthen family bonds because they decided to wait for death in Jamaica.

My grandmother claimed Grandad confided in her and said "I want to die and be buried at home, on my land."

If it was honored in his death, I would believe Grandma's claims. If it was honored, maybe I wouldn't label his death suicide by old age.

I cried in a dark corner in my hotel room as my boyfriend watched in horror. He's so supportive. I couldn't pray for a better support system than the one he provides. He's my sanity. His words usually ease every pain, but today, everything he said to me went in one ear and out the other. I'm sure his words of encouragement are somewhere fueling my will to go on, but it wasn't until I heard my father's voice that the room stopped spinning.

It took me three phone calls to get to my father. When he called me back, I went from 25-year-old underwriting professional to a toddler who needed her dad.

I never thought this day would come — me needing comfort from my father. I spent five years of my life suppressing that need. I didn't replace him with a father figure because I don't believe in that. A father figure is a man that acts as an example of what a man and father should be. A father figure creates the standard; good or bad. He wasn't the father I deserved, but he was still mine. In his faults I declared what I would not settle for in a man and designed my own standard for the type of man I want the father of my children to be.

"Dad, Granddad died and I don't know what to do. There's so much pressure to keep it together and just…"

"Mama, listen. You don't have to do anything. I'm sorry that he's passed, but he lived a good life. He did everything he wanted to do and everything is going to be alright," he said.

I remember that conversation because it was the realest response to death I've ever heard. My father was able to describe my grandfather's legacy in a way that made me feel he accomplished all that he needed to here on Earth and I should be proud of him.

Nyasia Draper

Bishop Elijah A. Trought lived by rules set by God. He would not compromise his faith nor would he abandon his principles under any circumstances. My grandfather was the thread that held the fabric of his families' sanity. He was a man who said very little, but meant so much to everyone who was blessed to know him.

I could no longer call to hear his voice nor could I go to his church in Brooklyn to feel his presence. The reconstruction of the church killed my grandfather way before his death. From the installation of flat screens where I grew up watching him sing along to hymns, to the destruction of the very pews he housed his bibles. Every essence of him and my childhood were erased.

With him, my willingness to put others before myself died. With him, my quarter-life crisis intensified and a piece of me was lying in a casket with him.

After speaking to my father, a switch went off. I detached myself from the situation so that I could be what I needed to be for my mother. I was no longer mourning the death of my grandfather, I was comforting a woman who lost her father.

I didn't have time to be Bishop Trought's granddaughter. I had to be Nadia's daughter. I didn't have time to miss him or go through old pictures only to realize there were only a few. I didn't have time to prepare to come face-to-face with the reality that he considered his family to be members of his church, not me. I didn't have time to reflect on the fact that I was a stranger at my grandfather's funeral. I barely knew the man that gave life to half of my world.

I finally got a hold of my mother. I took the phone call in the bathroom because I knew emotions were going to appear and I'm not one to display vulnerability. .

"I don't have any memories of him. We didn't go on family trips or anything like that. He was so wrapped up in the church he didn't spend time with his children. I don't want that for us," I recall her saying.

She went on to discuss the array of emotions she was feeling: guilt, anger, disappointment, defeat and sadness. She felt the relationship she had with her father didn't reach its full potential.

In the middle of my tears and my mother's rambling, the mental switch that went off earlier in the day seemed to be settling. It wasn't a switch that momentarily silenced my own pain. It was switch that turned off my humanity.

Have you ever watched Vampire Diaries? When a vampire could no longer withstand the emotions associated with engaging in mortal relationships, they would turn off their humanity. As a result, they were able to do whatever they desired without considering others. They were numb to consequences and free from thinking of anyone outside of themselves. True selfishness.

That is where I was.

CHAPTER 7

I tried to enjoy my Florida trip as much as I could. Going back home wasn't going to be healthy for me and I had a business trip planned upon my return. Luckily, in Jamaica it takes weeks to conduct a proper burial, so the illusion of normalcy continued.

It was my first time going to Universal Studios. I was like a kid in a candy store. Everything was so vibrant and serene. It filled my heart up with so much joy. The happiness I was feeling was at war with my grief. I often asked my boyfriend "Do you think it's messed up that I'm here? Shouldn't I be sad somewhere?"

I began to seclude myself.

"He's gone. My grandfather is gone," I thought.

My mind was scattered and my mother never called to ask me if I was okay. Instead, she called me and asked why I didn't call to check up on her. That alone shows you the dynamic of our relationship. I don't blame her though — I never let her know how I was really doing. She had enough on her plate.

I would be lying if I said the call didn't infuriate me. Such selfishness is usually ignored, but I couldn't ignore it this time. How could you call someone who has equally lost someone they loved to complain that they haven't checked up on you? At what point did our roles reverse? I love my mother dearly, but I needed a mother at that time and she needed a friend. She needed someone to comfort her and be sensitive to her needs. I don't know when I became just her friend and not her daughter, but it took that phone call to help me realize I hated it.

I didn't match her selfishness with the scolding it deserved. It wasn't worth the added stress.

I wasn't handling Granddad's death well. I didn't eat much. The relationship I had with food was unmatched and the sight of it disgusted me. It wasn't until my stomach tried to detach itself from my body that I realized it was imperative that I ate. I was surrounded by my boyfriend and his family who tried to convince me to eat every chance they saw a restaurant, but I didn't hear them. I couldn't hear anything outside of my own thoughts.

I felt naked. I felt broken. I felt like a walking spectacle and all the people around me wanted to do was comfort me, but I didn't want comfort. With comfort comes realizing that you are weak. With comfort comes the realization that you need someone else and relying on someone wasn't a part of my schedule.

Granddad dying was not a part of the schedule.

A few weeks went by and it was time to go to Jamaica. On the morning of my flight I had an anxiety attack. I don't know if it was because I woke up quickly and it shocked my system or if it was because I had been living in a false reality and getting on that plane confirmed Granddad was dead. I was traveling to burry my grandfather, alone. I had no preconceived notions of how I would handle it.

My mother couldn't make the trip for various reasons. First, it wasn't in my younger brother's best interest to be away from her for days at a time considering his diagnosis. We couldn't bring all of my brothers because none of them had passports and it would be too costly. Secondly, it was this ongoing tale that my presence was more needed than my mother's because I was my grandmother's golden egg. Apparently, nothing compared to comfort from the only granddaughter in the family. Lastly, my mother's request for a passport was denied. She was born in England, but had a valid green card. Despite the emergency, immigration rejected her request.

Per usual, I called my boyfriend in between my hyperventilating, he eased my mind, and I went about my day.

Jamaica was terrible. The house was filled with people I didn't know that refused to leave. My aunt Pearl hosted a booze fest we all knew my grandfather wouldn't have approved of and I spent the majority of my time trying to avoid being my mother's eyes and ears while she was in New York. My grandmother wanted me to sleep in her bed with her, the same bed my grandfather died in, and that was my final straw. It was overwhelming. I couldn't process my emotions and now, after seeing his cold body in an elaborate coffin, I just couldn't stay in that house anymore. Hours after his funeral, I changed my flight and left.

I could tell it hurt my grandmother's feelings. She always thinks someone's actions are a direct reflection of something she did, but in this case, I could no longer be strong for her. Instead of breaking down in front of her, I decided to go home and finally mourn the death of my grandfather.

When I got back from Jamaica, my mother and I got into a disagreement about my car. I left it under her care and someone decided to drag a key through it. I wasn't blaming her for it, but I was emotional. This was the second time someone keyed my car. My car was all I had.

As I cried looking at the damage, my mother trivialized my feelings. She used that time to be sensitive about my tone of voice. Coming home to my damaged car after a solo trip to bury my grandfather plus her need to make my emotional breakdown about her, lead to months of silence.

Nyasia Draper

I didn't get a chance to tell my mother how horrible Jamaica was. I didn't get a chance to tell her how hard it was to watch my grandmother cry out for her husband or that the people around her focused on how they could benefit from his death. We didn't speak on how even in her time of need, in *our* time of need, Grandma chose her church family over me. We didn't discuss how disgusting it was that the family, including my mother, was focused on years of hurt feelings and using this time to compete in a game of who's the better Trought.

I didn't show her any pictures of the elaborate production my aunt prepared for the funeral nor did I get to express how fucked up it was that she requested that I take pictures of the body. The only thing we got to discuss was how I changed my flight in the middle of the night and within hours she needed to come pick me up from the airport.

I was going through a whirlwind of emotions. Instead of comforting me, my mother drove off. She left me crying in the middle of the street. There was no way I was going to stay home under those circumstances. I left the funeral pamphlets and memorabilia on her bed and sped to Jennifer's house.

On the drive there I thought "What the fuck is wrong with her? How could she not see an issue with what she's doing?" I knew we we're both going through a difficult time, but when did pain become something only she could feel?

See, outside of grief, I was angry. I bought that car after Larry bought me a lemon and refused to help me repair it after agreeing to do so. My boyfriend refused to act as a cosigner for a potential new car, a decision his father made for him, and my mother tried to convince me I couldn't afford it.

"Car note? Car insurance? New York plates? Ha!"

Everyone doubted me and I persevered. I not only could afford a new car, I could afford my dream car with all the bells and whistles my naysayers wished they had.

With all of these thoughts running through my head, I was magically parked in front of Jennifer's house. I don't remember making any turns or stopping at any lights.

As I tearfully vented to her about my day, she immediately knew my pain was deeper than a keyed car. I didn't have to lay it all out for her. She just knew. In that moment, I wish my mother saw me through Jennifer's eyes.

Ending my relationship with people regardless of the nature of the relationship is easy for me. I didn't allow negativity in my life regardless of who was perpetuating it. Mother or not, my world was in shambles and I didn't need an additional blow.

Keeping me first, I loved my mother from a distance.

CHAPTER 8

Even though I was still under probation at my job, they were willing to grant me bereavement leave. Little did I know this gesture was the first and last sign of good faith. They fired me a month later.

Yup! The company that told me I was doing a great job, showed concern when my grandfather passed and continued to kiss my ass when asked for constructive criticism fired me. There was no explanation.

I later found out it wasn't personal. Their New York branch was an unsuccessful experiment and I was collateral damage.

This was the climax of my quarter-life crisis.

From that day forth, I was not going to be the woman my boyfriend loved and he was not going to be able to reel me back in. I was living in the hidden consciousness of my rebellious mind. I was losing myself.

The mental switch that went off in my head-on that dark night in Florida suddenly went from subtle to blatant. It somehow created a realm of consciousness that harnessed my willingness to succeed and produced a fuck-it mentality. All of my energy was dedicated to protecting the illusion of being numb.

I didn't send out one resume. I took this time of despair as a sign that I needed to slow down and enjoy my time off. I wanted to focus my energy on rediscovering what I wanted in life. I also wanted to enjoy myself. Have a little fun and create moments instead of waiting for them to appear.

My mother and I weren't talking, and I was going through medical issues that I, as a child, needed my mother to hold my hand through. Alas, I held my own.

I was 25 years old, unemployed and my grandfather died just shy of the anniversary of my stepfather's death.

I lost 10 pounds doing nothing. It was the benefit of being stressed out. I've been working out for months and couldn't shake the weight off, but good ol' quarter-life crisis took care of that. It was the only light in a dark tunnel.

My newfound freedom gave me time to do the things I couldn't do while I was employed full time. I went to the Made in America festival in Philadelphia with less than a day's notice, got lost in amazement watching Usher perform at Powerhouse midweek and partied at secret locations with celebrities into the wee hours of the morning. I even went on an unwarranted shopping spree. Doesn't sound like much, but spending money on anything outside of necessities was out of my character.

I was having the time of my life. No expectations. No responsibilities. No schedule.

Although I was unemployed, I wasn't broke. I didn't plan on losing my job, but I did have a savings account that could support my freedom while ensuring no bill was left unpaid.

I never had nothing to worry about before. I had just lost everything, but I was walking around like I just hit the lottery.

"I don't like this, Miss," said my mother.

Nyasia Draper

"Don't like what, Ma?" I replied.

My mother and I hadn't spoken in months. I was emotionally exhausted and knew distance was the only way to survive at the time. With her birthday approaching, I put my feelings aside to celebrate her. A "Happy Birthday Ma," turned into a reconciliation. We discussed what transpired and vowed to communicate better in the future. It was the first time I admitted to feeling like a forgotten child. Since the talk, my mother was extra attentive. I don't know if it was out of guilt or if it was genuine, but I appreciated it.

"This! You're not working. Every time I turn around you're running the streets. Sleeping all day, out all night. I don't know what's going on with you, but I don't like it."

I didn't give a shit.

I had a few moments where I thought my actions were counterproductive to everything I promised my teenage self. I even felt guilty that I was somehow using my grandfather's death as an excuse to live up to my full bum potential. I even sat down with my boyfriend and explained to him that I feared who I was becoming.

DEAR 25

I felt out of control. I had no direction. I stayed up all night and slept all day because my mind never shut down. I ran the streets in hopes that it would tire me out. I lost weight because I had no appetite. I didn't plan for a future because I wasn't sure what my future should be. Every day was an out-of-body experience. It was like I was trying to crawl back into my skin, but it kept rejecting me.

As depressing as it sounds, my misery created my happiness.

The new me wasn't planning her life. She wasn't applying for jobs or obsessing about the feelings of others. She was just gone. When I wasn't trying to crawl my way back to myself, I was watching myself live.

This new me wasn't me acting out because I lost the pillar of my family, it was to honor him. It was to shake loose all of the negative vibes my family was wallowing in after his death. I wasn't going to be depressed and regretful like they were. I was going to live my life for me, just like my grandfather did.

When Granddad died I no longer felt chained to my family. I was no longer obligated to deal with people I didn't want to deal with just to make his life easier. I didn't have to reprimand anyone for their inadequate ability to properly care for him. I didn't need to worry about how my actions would determine anyone's blood pressure.

Granddad died happy. Granddad died on his terms. I wanted to be like Granddad. I wanted to watch my life flash before my eyes and grin from ear to ear like he did that day we sat on the veranda in Jamaica.

CHAPTER 9

I went from feeling like an unaccomplished, unrealistic millennial to feeling like I had a new hold on life. Three months passed since the climax of my quarter-life crisis. I decided to try to weasel my way back into the job market. I was applying to corporate communications, underwriting and editorial positions. I figured I had nothing to lose so why not chase my dreams despite the lack of financial promise.

With every job application came a sense of familiarity. I was becoming me again, but without the urgency of becoming the woman I imagined myself to be. Instead of thinking I was running out of time, I realized you aren't supposed to have all your ducks in a row by 25.

I wish I had someone tell me it was okay to enjoy your twenties. I wish someone told me that most adults haven't established what their standards were much less tried to meet those standards at this stage. I wish I knew that being 25 years old did not mean my clock was running out, but that it was just starting. I wish someone told my elders to respect my process — to respect *our* process.

Respect that being 25 years old in 2016 has a different meaning than being 25 years old in 1962. Times are different and priorities have evolved.

The roads traveled through life are your own. No matter who you may have by your side or what redirected your journey, you are the only one making strides in your shoes. You have to make your own decisions and travel using your own moral compass. The definition of success, happiness and family is subjective.

The generations before me give millennials a hard time. They say we are entitled; they say we don't value marriage; they say we are the reason why there is a decline in the population. It took me losing myself to realize those aren't accusations based on truths. I didn't realize how much millennials were mistrusted until I ignored the expectations of my elders and began following my own path.

DEAR 25

We're not entitled. We went through the necessary channels to obtain the qualifications for the careers the generation before us suggested. We have the degrees. We've completed internship programs. We even have recommendation letters. Unfortunately, that isn't enough. Every time we get close to the finish line, those who are in position to declare us winners move it further — just enough to discourage us, but close enough to keep us interested in the race.

We do value marriage. We refuse to settle for the first person with similar interests just to fulfill our parents' dreams of becoming grandparents. Marriage isn't a business. It isn't a piece of paper that deems us better than those without it nor should it overshadow individuality. We value connections. We value being in relationships that will stand the test of time and not the test of patience.

Building a family isn't something to play with. We aren't reproducing solely to extend legacies. We want to raise healthy, independent, mentally stable individuals. How you raise your children begins with who you decided to raise your children with.

Nyasia Draper

Some of us loathe at the thought of becoming parents. Yes, populating the Earth is important, but it isn't everyone's responsibility. Forcing that ideology on others creates room for resentment between children and their parents. It is unhealthy for a child to feel unwanted or for a parent to feel inept. Those who are unfit are forced to raise children who are at times forced into dysfunction because of it. Is society really willing to sacrifice mental health for an increased population?

It sounds hypocritical to abandon my obsession with scheduling when my advice to others is to be calculated in your decisions.

Throughout my quarter-life crisis I learned it was important to be prepared, but even more important to be flexible in your approach. There are a multitude of ways to reach your goals. Sometimes you have the right strategy, but you don't give yourself enough time to see your strategy work.

CHAPTER 10

Flexibility lead me to a job fair. The traditional approach to finding employment wasn't working and I made yet another birthday promise.

"Through hell or high water I am going to be on somebody's beach for my 26th birthday," I typed in the group chat.

Spending my birthday on a vacation was my victory lap. To be somewhere tropical on my birthday meant I won and my quarter-life crisis loss. It meant I was stronger than the year before. I fought my way back to Nyasia.

The job fair was filled with companies I had no interest in, but I shook hands, left resumes, and assured the recruiters that I was prepared to work within their company as they saw fit. I wasn't looking for a specific position. I was looking for a salary that would put my ass on a beach come March.

As I worked my way around the room I noticed a well-known publication amongst those hiring. I'd been applying online for years and couldn't land an interview. There was no way I was going to forfeit face-to-face contact with a company I've tried years to work for.

I introduced myself and informed the hiring manager of the positions I've previously applied to on the company's job board.

The recruiter glanced over my resume and asked if I had any writing samples. I explained that I'd been published for both print and digital publications and I was more than happy to forward my work to her.

She proceeded to hand me her business card and requested that I send her a link to my portfolio.

I didn't have a portfolio. I was advised to create a portfolio by my previous editor, but I never saw the point. If you googled my name, all of my work came up.

Duh.

I nodded my head and thanked her for her time. I knew that if I didn't act quickly I would always doubt what could've happened if I had a portfolio.

I rushed home that day and created a portfolio within the hour. My portfolio included six article clippings on my own website that depicted my versatility, knowledge on trending topics, and the ability to create original content. I emailed the recruiter and specified that I was interested in the digital media manager position.

I didn't get the job.

Instead, she thought I would be a better fit in a non-managerial role, as a researcher. I accepted the offer without hesitation. The schedule wasn't your typical nine to five, but I didn't care. I was now a researcher for a reputable publication. I was getting my quarter-life crisis the fuck up out of here.

To be honest, I didn't understand why she pegged me for the job. I didn't have a librarian degree nor had I acted solely as a fact-checker for my previous employers. I mean, yes, I have fact-checked information and analyzed documents for accuracy before, but I never thought it would translate as a researcher for a publication. Nonetheless, I was grateful.

Scheduling my life taught me how to crash without burning. Me not getting the position I wanted was the crash. The opportunity to still work for a publication I respected was "without burning."

The old me would've broke out in hives and eaten myself into a coma while watching an SVU marathon. I was making progress. I was able to acknowledge an opportunity within an unfavorable situation and remain positive. I was changing for the better.

I was no longer an optimistic pessimist. I was aware that things may not go as planned, but I wasn't waiting for a disappointment to happen. I was managing my anxiety better and I was a better person because of it. Change is good. Change is constant. Change shouldn't be treated as something that occurs after a disaster happens. Change is the result of progress.

I outgrew my own negativity.

DEAR 25

Turns out waiting for the wrong things to happen can sometimes produce negativity. When you assume the worst you are blinded by negativity so much so that when good things happen, you can't identify with it. You can't appreciate it. You spend so much time preventing the worst things from happening your mind is incapable of being excited for the good.

It's an unhealthy perspective that can lead to stress, hypertension, insomnia and so much more. Why kill yourself waiting for the worst to happen when you're surrounded by so much beauty? I worked hard to create a safe space for myself, but my optimistic pessimism blinded me from realizing what I'd accomplished thus far.

I loved my new job. I was getting paid to be a professional creep. I used to sit at home scrolling through social media and blogs trying to find out the latest news on celebrities; in my new job, I got to use my investigative skills to inform the public about pressing issues and things that were going on in their communities.

Nyasia Draper

It made me feel important. It reintroduced me to my purpose. It reminded me why I went to school to study communications. It put me back on track emotionally and financially, and I will forever be indebted to this experience.

CHAPTER 11

"Hey Mama, what you got planned for your birthday?" my dad said.

"I'm going to the Dominican Republic," I replied.

"You just got a job and now you're going to the Dominican Republic? You was just broke last week. Man I tell you, boy," he laughed.

My father hated that I had a passion for travel. Between him almost being denied re-entry into the country during his honeymoon to those damn Taken movies, he was not enthused with my need to see the world. My mother on the other hand, she didn't care where I went as long as it was a maximum of four days and she could get in contact with me.

Nyasia Draper

I booked a superior, deluxe room at Be Live, an all-inclusive resort in Puerto Plata, Dominican Republic, for four days. I was arriving on the morning of my birthday and planning a candlelight dinner that evening. It was time to celebrate how far I'd come.

My birthday is in March. I never considered myself a winter baby, but that changed when a snowstorm forced the cancellation of all flights from New York on my birthday. My flight was cancelled and so was my birthday.

For my birthday, I went to work and let my quarter-life crisis dance around my cubicle singing "nanana boo boo, you can't shake me." Family and friends sent celebratory messages and I was disgusted.

Happy Birthday?! What's so happy about it? Do you see clear skies and sandy beaches? Oh. Ok.

Your birthday is supposed to be a day to appreciate where you've been, celebrate what you've accomplished, and welcome 365 more days to continue your progress. Every birthday I set goals. I had a lot to overcome this time around. I was hoping the one day that's designated for me would be enjoyable.

I had been through so much. I just wanted to put it all behind me. I was ready to move on. This trip meant I was ready. It was my version of reverse psychology. I figured if I told myself I was ok, then I would be.

A quarter-life crisis isn't supposed to spill into your 26th year. For my 25th birthday I didn't do much because I was already heading down a dark emotional path. The goal was to stray from that path by my next birthday and so far, it was looking like I was going to fail.

After self-reflecting, I realized I could still be victorious. I had faced my fears head-on and learned new things about myself. Life got the best of me at times, but it was short lived because I refused to succumb to it. My victory lap was postponed, but it was still warranted. I still won one of the biggest battles of my life against my biggest opponent — me. I can still overcome the year of loss, disappointments and confusion. Okay, the 'Fuck You 25' party was postponed. So, what! Tomorrow is another day and there is another day after that.

I spent days on the phone with Expedia trying to find a new flight and check the availability of my superior room. From being placed on hold for three hours to being told the hotel wasn't communicating well with the Expedia representatives, I was determined to run my victory lap.

After three days, I was on the first flight out of New York to Puerto Plata.

Puerto Plata was better than I imagined. The weather wasn't too hot. The island breeze didn't cause chills. The decor was like a tight hug from a spa, and the ambiance was inviting. Check-in was a bit lengthy, but I didn't complain because it gave me a chance to appreciate the sounds of the waterfall and the backdrop of the mountains. The staff made sure I was well cared for and my superior, deluxe room was spotless.

I won.

CHAPTER 12

I won. Not because I survived the trials and tribulations of adulthood, but because I was able to let go of who I thought I was in order to become who I am today. My inner child was crushed, but not broken, and for that, I am thankful for my quarter-life crisis.

I am thankful that my world crashed before my feet. As I walked through the shattered glass to safety, I sliced open my feet and bled out all the false promises scheduling my life had given me.

There is no solution when you don't realize you are the problem. You can't discover what makes you happy if you're denying that you're miserable.

I was the problem.

I put so much pressure on myself. I didn't realize I

was crushing my own spirit. My expectations, although reasonable, were so high it made me feel small. I hated accomplishing little things that led to the bigger picture. I stayed in the dark glimpsing at a light that seemed light-years away, not realizing I put the damn light there and I could easily bring it closer.

I've learned to get out of my own way. I've learned to create a space where I can enjoy the journey without losing sight of my destination.

I've learned I need to acknowledge what I'm feeling, when I'm feeling it. Hiding my emotions from others is one thing, but disguising them from myself is unhealthy. I was so focused on getting over the hardships in my life, I didn't give myself time to get through them.

Dear 25, you've given me something I didn't know I lost. You've shown me the beauty in my struggles, given me the patience for uncertainty and prepared me to face whatever comes next. I did not know it at the time, but I know now that you were just an inner battle I had to face.

You were inevitable.

Luckily, you arrived at 25, but you could've easily

showed up at 18 or even 50. Granted, you'd have a different title, but your impact would remain the same.

You were the elders telling me I didn't work hard enough even when I surpassed their expectations. You took Larry away to help me understand what he meant to my family even if he didn't mean the same to me. You took my grandfather's life to remind me to live mine. You rattled my relationship with my mother to help me realize vulnerability is not a handicap and it's okay to be selfish. It's okay to put your well-being above others even when their livelihoods are contingent on your selflessness.

You took me on an emotional roller-coaster to show me it's okay to have feelings. You made the very person who broke my heart put it back together again to teach me how to forgive. You left me unemployed to grant me the time I needed to pay attention to the lessons you continue to bring me. You changed pessimistic optimism into peaceful self-love.

To the witnesses of 25, I ask for your patience and understanding. Know that the process you are witnessing isn't something you can control, but something you can be in support of. You are appreciated even if it is not expressed. You are not at fault as this battle is not a battle for two. You couldn't prevent this from happening nor is this process a resistance to your love. I am sorry because I don't have a guide for you.

Dear 25ers, you and I are one in the same. We may not deal with our issues the same way and we may not come from the same family dynamic, but at some point we felt lost. At some point, you looked in the mirror and didn't recognize who you were and had no direction as to who you were becoming.

It is a difficult emotion to express. It's a painful process to endure. It's something you will survive.

I commend you for getting through it even if you are just beginning because I have faith in your strength. I'm excited to see what your quarter-life crisis will reveal to you. I am sorry because I know at times you will feel alone in this world and I can't be there to tell you you're not.

I look forward to hearing about the experiences your carefree attitude lead to and what event helped you realize it was time to deal with what was going on in your

DEAR 25

life rather than run from it. I look forward to hearing how you defend your victory lap and just how good it felt to look in the mirror and be happy with the person looking back at you.

And it may seem crazy to say, but if you've gotten to the other side of any hardship you know why I have to say thank heavens for 25!

xoxo Nyasia

www.ingramcontent.com/pod-product-compliance
Lightning Source LLC
Chambersburg PA
CBHW051955290426
44110CB00015B/2254